STEAM SHED
Portrait

H.G. Forsythe
Atlantic

THE AUTHOR

H. G. Forsythe has been taking pictures
of trains since he was eight. Australian by
birth, he came to England in the early
fifties and set about recording the steam
scene, first with an ancient Rolleiflex,
then a Leica I I If. He is a professional
writer, photographer and scientific
consultant. His railway articles first
appeared in that 'best of all boy's papers'
'Meccano Magazine' and since then have
been published in the transport press
throughout the world.

ACKNOWLEDGMENTS

The author wishes to thank Mr John
Edgington, Technical Information
Officer of the National Railway Museum;
Mr Peter Hands, author and publisher of
the 'What happened to steam' series for
providing many useful historical facts,
and Messrs Jack Gardner and Peter
Townend of British Rail for remembering
so many fascinating facets of steam lore.
Grateful thanks are also due to many
others, too numerous to mention, who
helped in compiling this book.

THE PHOTOGRAPHS

All photographs in this book date from
1956—65 and were taken by the author
unless otherwise credited.

DESIGN Nigel Trevena

PRINTED BY Century Litho
Falmouth, Cornwall

© H. G. Forsythe 1981
First published 1981

Published by
ATLANTIC BOOKS
25 Scorrier Street St Day Redruth Cornwall
Telephone (0209) 821016

ISBN 0 906899 02 8

Keeping them running

There was something alive, something almost human about the steam locomotive. Individuals every one, members of the same class — seemingly identical in every way — could be as different as any two people, and could vary from day to day. Engines had their moods. Writing in *The Locomotive* for November 1927, that distinguished engineer, E. A. Phillipson, said: 'The mere fact that the locomotive is customarily referred to as a 'she' has no doubt prepared misogynist entrants to the profession for her fickle vagaries. Whilst many theories have been advanced for variations in performance, none has yet been satisfactorily substantiated.'

And, indeed, those great ladies required the constant attentions of an an army of attendants, no less than any courtesan. Although a very simple machine compared with the modern diesel, the steam locomotive did need a great deal of attention to keep it functioning properly. Regular visits to the motive power depots for servicing and maintenance were essential and it was in those engine sheds that so much of the true atmosphere of steam, existed and where the unique and now vanished lives of the men who tended steam could be seen.

In both the works, where locomotives were built and overhauled, and in the running sheds, where they were kept going, there existed a whole host of crafts, skills and arts — now, sadly, almost gone for ever. These were dusty and dirty, smoky and dark places — if you visited them you came away with that characteristic, unforgettable smell of steam, oil and cinders clinging to your clothes. Yet to those with the eye to see — and the camera to record — the locomotive sheds were filled with the true spirit and adventure of the railway. It was there that the railwaymen cared for those great machines and kept our railway system operating. It was often filthy and unpleasant work, and by the early nineteen-fifties it was becoming more and more difficult to find men willing to work under such conditions. The end of steam, as we knew it, was being forced on the railway by labour problems just as much as economic ones.

They have gone now, those halls of the giants. With the end of steam most have vanished without trace, others are clean and tidy beyond recognition and cater for the new types of motive power. With them, too, has vanished a great and proud tradition; a part of our industrial heritage. It is to record some of that great heritage, which was fully extant only twenty years ago, and as a tribute to steam railway men and their machines, that this book has been compiled.

Phillipson was more prophetic than he knew when he speculated back in 1928, again in *The Locomotive*: 'It is difficult to forecast the direction which will be taken to provide the railway with novel means of propulsion. Purely as a flight of fancy it is suggested that, the scientists having successfully harnessed the power of the mighty atom, we shall see the 'Cornish Riviera Limited' start away from Paddington at an incredible rate of acceleration with an engine having the dimensions of a postage stamp tucked away in an odd corner of the guard's van.' Well, the HST has an incredible rate of acceleration, but so far as personality is concerned, compared with an A4 or a Castle in full flight, perhaps Phillipson's guard's van analogy isn't so far out after all.

LEFT: *Suffering from a leaky inside steam pipe joint, Castle Class No.5087* Tintern Abbey *storms into Sonning Cutting on New Year's Eve 1962.*
TITLE PAGE: *A summer Saturday at Willesden shed, 1962.*
OUTSIDE COVERS: *Panoramic view of King's Cross 'Top Shed' in 1958.*

1

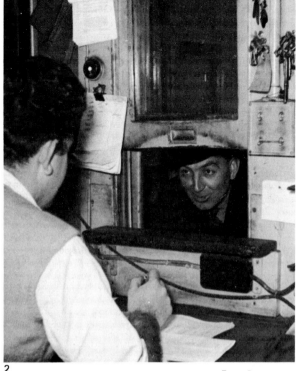

2

3

5

6

7

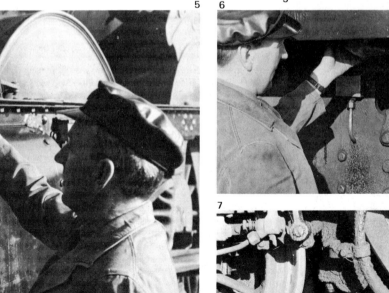

Collecting a 'Castle'

1 A fine morning in 1961, and Driver Jack Gardner arrives at Reading (WR) Shed for his turn of duty. His locomotive, Castle Class No.5076 *Gladiator* is already in steam and waiting for her driver and fireman outside the running shed.

2 Jack first books on for duty with Barry Smith, Time Clerk at Reading Shed. Then it will be over to the locomotive where Jack will unlock the tool boxes and collect the oil cans to take over to Stores.

3 At Stores, Jack collects cylinder lubricating oil. On the left, the smaller can contains paraffin and a still larger can, to be passed through next, contains general lubricating oil.

4 Starting on the tender, Jack oils one of the axle boxes. Always a railway enthusiast, these days Jack is a Traction Inspector, still based at Reading, and in his own time he is Diesel Inspector for the Severn Valley Railway and Steam Inspector at the GWS depot, Didcot.

5 Oiling *Gladiator's* left hand outside valve spindle front end.

6 Here Jack oils the knuckle joint of the rocking arm to the inside valve spindle. In the Castle, of course, the inside one drives the outside spindle through the rocking lever.

7 In the pit under *Gladiator*, Jack is oiling the bogie axle box. Steam locomotives had innumerable oiling points and it was essential for drivers to know every single one of them.

8 While his fireman is getting onto the footplate on the opposite side, Jack pulls the water column around to top up the tender. This column is fitted with the newer rubber flexible bags in place of the old leather type.

9 Ready to back off shed, today *Gladiator* is diagrammed to work forward from Reading the cross country South of England to Birkenhead train, popularly known as 'The Continental' amongst shed staff. With through coaches from Eastbourne, Hastings, Ramsgate, Margate, Folkestone, Deal, Dover, Sandwich and Brighton, it has been assembled at Redhill and is scheduled to leave Reading at 1.07 pm.

4

8 9

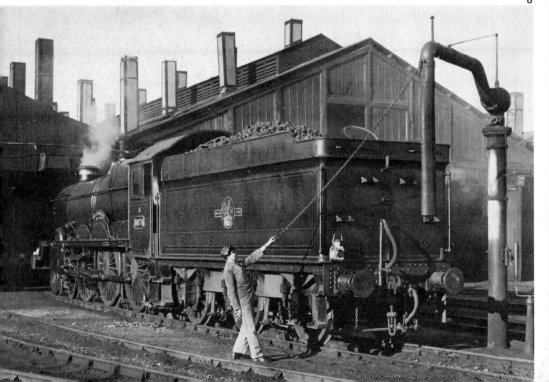

Reading WR

The original broad gauge shed at Reading opened in March 1840 and was situated immmediately opposite the old station. In 1880, the standard gauge locomotive shed was opened, its site being in the fork of the main lines to Bristol and Plymouth. The original layout of Reading Station survived almost to the end of the century, the present station being opened in 1898.

Reading shed was initially a roundhouse, with a central turntable. This survived until 1930, when it was rebuilt as a straight-through running shed. A repair shop was built in 1932 and the MPD remained virtually unchanged up to closure in January 1965.

ABOVE LEFT: Castle No.5076 *Gladiator* resting one frosty night in 1961 in the yard at Reading MPD. A certain cleaner at Reading took the greatest pride in turning out his engines looking impeccable, and often added extra unofficial embellishments of his own, like the painted smokebox door hinges, lamp brackets and lifeguard irons on 5076. *Gladiator* was built in 1938, withdrawn in 1964 and scrapped by Hayes, Bridgend. 'The Continental' was a regular turn for this engine. Interestingly, the Southern loco working from Redhill was turned and serviced at the GWR shed rather than Reading Southern Shed. The return working left Reading at 1.29 pm, only 32 minutes after the loco's scheduled arrival, so it was quicker and more convenient for it to drop down to the GWR shed.

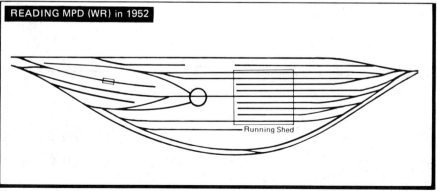

READING MPD (WR) in 1952

Running Shed

ALLOCATIONS at READING WR (81D) End 1959			
4300 Class 2-6-0	**2800 Class 2-8-0**	**Hall 4-6-0**	**6100 Class 2-6-2T**
6302	2841	4913	6101
6313	2853	4977	6103
6324	3858	4987	6104
7331	*Total 3*	4989	6107
Total 4		4993	6112
		4998	6122
Castle 4-6-0	**Mod. Hall 4-6-0**	5901	6130
4086	6960	5906	6131
4092	6968	5907	6134
5018	7906	5915	6153
5036	7914	5936	6161
5076	7919	5957	6168
Total 5	*Total 5*	5979	*Total 12*
		5982	
		5993	
		6953	
		Total 16	

RIGHT:
At most MPD's fitters worked around the clock. At Reading, Eric Hall (left) and George Stares work on Hall Class 4-6-0 No.5906 *Lawton Hall*. Eric is drilling out a defective cylinder head stud. The replacement stud can be seen on the front footplate near the left hand end of the spanner.

BELOW RIGHT:
Fireman Eddie Robinson of Reading Shed fills the oil head-lamp of Worcester-based Modified Hall No.6989 *Wightwick Hall*, in preparation for a late night turn of duty. Many years ago, in one of his verses for children, E.V. Lucas wrote about the fireman or 'stoker':

The Stoker stands by the engine fire,
And feeds the flames to their full desire;
At night he opens the furnace door,
And the train tears by with a glare and a roar;
He oils the engine from time to time,
And covers himself with grease and grime,
Then cleans his hands in an absent way,
On a piece of rag as dirty as they,
An engine stoker I'd like to be,
Except for the trouble of washing for tea.

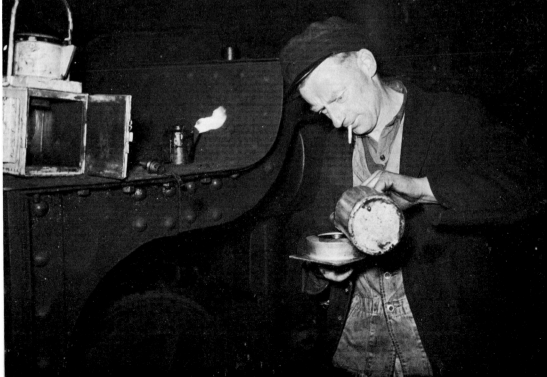

5700 Class 0-6-0PT	9400 Class 0-6-0PT
3723	8430
3738	9447
4609	*Total 2*
4641	
4661	**1400 Class 0-4-2T**
4665	1407
4670	*Total 1*
7788	
9749	**2251 Class 0-6-0**
9763	2212
9791	2245
Total 11	2262
	3216
	Total 4
5600 Class 0-6-2T	
6654	
Total 1	*TOTAL 64*

Old Oak Common

Old Oak Common was opened on 17th March 1906. Designed by G.J. Churchward, it was the largest GWR motive power depot, measuring 444 ft by 360 ft and containing four 65 ft turntables, each with 28 radiating roads, making a total of 112 engine pits. It was the prototype internal turntable type of depot - similar designs were used all over the GWR system but none was as large.

On the eastern side there was a lifting and repair shop with 12 pits and a traverser outside. All the usual support of fitters, machinists, smiths, coppersmiths, carpenters and so on, together with their equipment, was provided. A block of offices at the south corner of the east wall was occupied in the 1950's by John Armstrong, Divisional Locomotive Superintendent, together with his staff.

Old Oak was situated three miles from Paddington on the up side of the line. It had superseded the sheds at Westbourne Park which had themselves superseded the original roundhouse at Bishop's Road in March 1855.

BELOW: The coal stage at Old Oak Common had elevated supply roads and was the GWR system's largest. Above was a 290,000 gallon water tank. The Great Western did not like mechanical coaling plants, preferring tip wagons which were hand filled so that coal supply could be selective and consistent. Express engines, like Castle Class No.5045 *Earl of Dudley*, would get the big pieces of first quality Welsh coal, the rest going to smaller and less important fry.

RIGHT: *Earl of Dudley's* smoke box is cleaned out with a steam hose attached to a small cock on the front of the smoke box while the coaling operation proceeds. No.5045 was a visitor from Stafford Road, Wolverhampton, and was withdrawn in September 1962, aged 26. Just behind, a visitor from St Philip's Marsh, No.5049 *Earl of Plymouth* awaits her turn.

The great shed at Old Oak Common was light and spacious. The A-type roof trusses were of 60 ft span, carried on long girders and supported by cast iron columns. There was extensive glazing and the 65 ft turntables were completely boarded over. There was plenty of electric lighting and ample ventilation.

Line up of resting steam on a Saturday in 1960. From left: an unidentified 4700 class 2-8-0; Castle Class No.4076 *Carmarthen Castle* (one of the originals built in 1924); No.6029 *King Edward VIII*; Grange Class No.6856 *Stowe Grange* and Castle Class No.5046 *Earl Cawdor*.

Boiler blow-down for Castle No.5014 *Goodrich Castle*. A long time Old Oak loco, No.5014 survived until 1965, spending her last few months at Tyseley. Note, on the extreme left, a fitter's portable work bench with, nearer left, a fitter's barrow with a hollow for carrying valves.

A Castle is turning on one of the shed turntables while a shed driver (left) chats to a fitter.

ABOVE: In Old Oak
repair shop, Castle Class
No.5071 *Spitfire* has lost
her front pair of driving
wheels and pony truck.
Note the built up crank
axle driven by the two
inside cylinders. These
axles were made up of
nine separate parts
hydraulically pressed
together and then keyed.
The extended webs were
for balancing. On the right,
Spitfire is seen supported
by jacks and blocks
while her front drivers
and motion are repaired.
A visitor to Old Oak,
No.5071 was based at
Gloucester (Horton Road)
and was withdrawn in
October 1963.

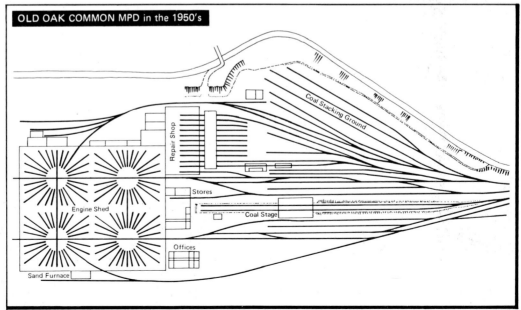

OLD OAK COMMON MPD in the 1950's

Coal Stacking Ground

Repair Shop

Engine Shed

Stores

Coal Stage

Offices

Sand Furnace

Diesels
D3597
D3598
D3599
D3600
D3601
D3602
D3604

1500 Class 0-6-0PT
1500
1503
1504
1505
Total 4

2251 Class 0-6-0
2276
2282
Total 2

5700 Class 0-6-0PT
3648
3688
3754
4615
4644
5717
5764
7722
8751
8753
8754
8756
8757
8759
8760
8762
8763
8764
8765
8767
8768
8770
8771
8772
8773
9658
9659
9661
9701
9702
9703
9704
9705
9706
9707
9709
9710
9751
9754
9758
9784
Total 41

Castle 4-6-0
4082
4096
5008
5014
5027
5034
5035
5040
5043
5044
5052
5056
5060
5065
5066
5074
5082
5084
5087
5093
7001
7004
7008
7010
7013
7017
7020
7024
7025
7027
7030
7032
7033
7036
Total 34

4700 Class 2-8-0
4700
4701
4702
4704
4708
Total 5

Hall 4-6-0
4919
5923
5929
5931
5932
5954
5958
5976
5987
6920
6942
Total 11

Mod Hall 4-6-0
6959
6961
6962
6966
6978
6990
7902
7903
7904
7927
Total 11

King 4-6-0
6000
6002
6003
6004
6009
6010
6012
6015
6018
6019
6021
6023
6024
6025
6028
6029
Total 16

6100 Class 2-6-2T
6110
6113
6120
6121
6132
6135
6141
6142
6144
6145
6158
6159
Total 12

9400 Class 0-6-0PT
9400
9405
9410
9411
9412
9414
9416
9418
9419
9420
9423
9469
9479
Total 13

BR 9F 2-10-0
92211
92229
92230
92238
92239
92240
92241
92244
92245
92246
92247
Total 11

TOTAL STEAM 160
TOTAL DIESEL 7

BELOW LEFT: A Fire Lighter at Old Oak, shovel filled with specially prepared bundles of wood and oily cotton waste, makes ready to start the lighting-up procedure on a Castle. Usually known as a 'lighter-up' from GWR days, he will allow about 5 hours for the Castle to raise steam, 3 hours for smaller engines. In addition to lighting up, he will keep a watchful eye on other engines standing in steam, regularly checking their water levels and the state of their fires.

BELOW RIGHT: A Boiler Smith's Mate checks the water level in the boiler of a locomotive, being refilled after a boiler washout. The gauges, of course, show no steam pressure and the regulator is fully open. It is important not to overfill the boiler and due allowance must be made for expansion which will occur after lighting up.

ABOVE: A summer Saturday afternoon at Old Oak Common. The running sheds are at right and the brick arches of the 1 in 50 ramp approach to the coal stage can be seen on the extreme right. The water columns still have old type teather bags in this 1961 picture. The 4300 Class Mogul (middle left) has a 3000 gallon tender - probably temporarily.

RIGHT: It is late on a summer Saturday afternoon and Castle Class No.5065 *Newport Castle* backs off shed. No.5065 was booked that day to work the 'Red Dragon' from Paddington to Swansea. The train originated around the turn of the century, leaving Paddington at 6.10 pm. At first unnamed, it was not until the autumn of 1950 that it received its attractive title. *Newport Castle* was withdrawn in early 1963 and scrapped 11 months later. Note the ringed signals. Drivers sometimes complained that their movement was so limited that it was often hard to see when they were off.

Camden

London's first main line terminus, Euston, was opened by the London and Birmingham Railway on 20th July 1837. The severe gradient from Regent's Canal into the terminus (1 in 68 and 1 in 77) was too much for the locomotives then in use and arrangements were made to haul trains up to Camden - 1½ miles from Euston - by continuous cables. These were powered by two Maudslay & Field condensing engines, sited underground immediately to the north of Regent's Canal Bridge. Trains were hauled to the top of the incline where locomotives, stabled at Camden, took over. In the reverse direction, engines were detached at Camden and the trains descended by gravity.

For the first few weeks after opening, the winding engines being not quite complete, a "powerful engine" was hired from Robert Stephenson & Co. of Newcastle, to act as banker up to Camden. Initial traffic was handled by the little Bury locomotives, also on hire.

Thus, from the beginning there was an engine shed at Camden. It was temporary at first, but permanent sheds were soon built on both sides of the line. According to official records, two were opened in early 1847, cable operations having ceased two and a half years earlier on.

TOP LEFT: The entrance to Camden Shed was near Chalk Farm, in Dumpton Place off Gloucester Road. The Coronation pacific is on her way to the ash plant.

BOTTOM LEFT: Enginemen check notices in the entrance to the administrative offices. Roster details, information about permanent way, speed restrictions and other important details were regularly posted and were required reading for crews.

July 14th 1844. The shed builders, Messrs Branson & Gwyther, were paid £61,715.2s.6d for the work. The 'Goods Engine House', constructed on the up side of the line, was the famous Round House. This was closed as a loco shed in the 1860's due to the continuing difficulty in finding paths for locos across the running lines. At first the building was a railway warehouse, then from 1871 Gilbey's leased it as a bonded store, using it right up to 1966. Today, the Round House is a theatre.

For years after the end of cable haulage, it was usual to pilot all trains out of Euston with an additional engine which was slipped and ran off on a siding at Camden in a hair-raising split-second dash. This practice ceased in 1869; amazingly there had been no serious mishaps.

With the closure of the Round House, the shed on the down side of the line became Euston's main depot. Camden MPD was always very cramped. Tucked away right next to the main line it was improved a little in 1901 and 1906 during widening of the cutting, and better access was provided. During the LMS shed re-organisation in the early 1930's, Camden was given up-to-date ash and mechanical coaling plants, but the shed remained cramped and engines had literally to squeeze past the entrance and administrative offices after turning and coaling and on their way to the ash pits.

Camden supplied express passenger locomotives for services out of Euston and many visiting engines were serviced there every day. In 1954, 55 engines were allocated to the MPD. When these pictures were taken, on Wednesday 12th August 1959, the allocation was 45, for by this time 1B was beginning to feel the impact of dieselisation and a modern diesel servicing shed was being built. A month later, nine locos were transferred away and nine more left before the end of that year. Closure to steam came on 9th September 1963 and the remaining four steam locos were all allocated to Willesden (1A). They were 2-6-2T No. 41239 and Coronation Class Pacifics Nos. 46239 City of Chester, 46240 City of Coventry and 46245 City of London. For a time, Camden shed remained in use as a diesel depot until demolition in 1964.

ABOVE: The modern ash lifting plant (at left), when working, and the narrow gauge trucks associated with it - running both in and beside the pits - usually enabled ashes from smoke- and fire-boxes to be disposed of quickly and easily. Today, the plant is out of order and shed staff are rapidly becoming overwhelmed by mountains of hot ash. A visitor from Longsight, Manchester (9A), No. 70033 *Charles Dickens*, looks on and, on the left, Royal Scot No.46155 *The Lancer* awaits attention.

RIGHT: At a busy MPD, engine movements have to be carefully planned. This is specially true where there is a straight-through running shed, as at Camden. Here, at the administrative offices, engine working arrangements are listed in full on the special blackboard.

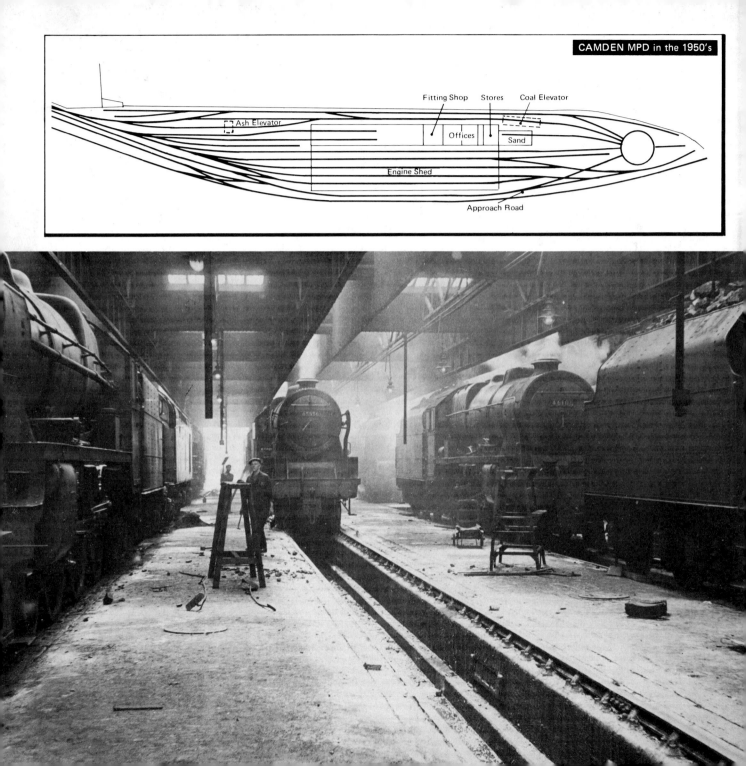

CAMDEN MPD in the 1950's

Fitting Shop   Stores   Coal Elevator

Ash Elevator

Offices

Sand

Engine Shed

Approach Road

LEFT: Inside Camden's running shed. Locomotives awaiting attention or their next spell of duty are stabled strictly in correct order. At left, one of the three English Electric Type 4's (now Class 40) then allocated to the depot stands behind a Royal Scot. Over the deep inpection pit in the middle stands rebuilt Patriot No.45536 *Private W. Wood VC*, visiting from Longsight, while on the right is Camden Royal Scot No.46101 *Royal Scots Grey*.

ABOVE: Polmodie (Glasgow) Coronation Pacific No.46222 *Queen Mary* will be leaving the shed soon to haul the 'Midday Scot' northwards. Dusty and dirty, she will remain that way at least till she gets home. Just now Camden has just two cleaners on the staff instead of the usual 32! *Queen Mary* was one of the original streamlined Pacifics, withdrawn in November 1963 and immediately scrapped at Crewe. Her train, the 'Midday Scot' received its official name in 1927 but the service had been running since 1889. In July 1893 it became one of the first LNWR expresses to be formed of corridor stock and was affectionately known as 'The Corridor' amongst railway staff.

LEFT: 'Jinty' 0-6-0T No.47668 emerges from Camden's mechanical coaling stage after taking on supplies. At Camden the coaling stage could only be reached via the 70 ft turntable, at least when travelling in the correct direction. The first mechanical coaling plant in Britain was built by the LNWR at Crewe North Shed in 1910. Note the line of coal waggons on the left. The leading one, immediately under the plant, is just about to be hoisted up to discharge its contents into the bunker.

At Camden, as at many other big urban sheds, a measure of coke was included with loco coal to help reduce smoke nuisance at the shed.

'Jinties' were the standard design of LMS shunting tank. Their attractive nickname was inherited from S.W. Johnson's 1883 Midland Railway 0-4-0 saddle tanks, so called because they had J class boilers. 422 of the latter day 'Jinties' were built between 1924 and 1931 and nine have been preserved, not including 47668.

BELOW: Royal Scot No.46126 *Royal Army Service Corps*, newly arrived at Camden after working the up 'Northern Irishman' from Carlisle, has her tender filled immediately after coaling. She will now proceed to the overworked ash plant to have her fire and smokebox cleaned.

ABOVE: Now over the ash pits, No.46126 has her hopper ash pan doors opened. Her fire will be thoroughly cleaned and the ash pan raked before the hopper doors are closed again. Note the fire cleaning tools on the ground, some welding equipment nearby and the pile of clinker in the left foreground.

ABOVE RIGHT: A rare visitor to Camden, a 9F 2-10-0, has her left big end oiled. 2-10-0's were rarely seen at Camden, being usually dealt with at Willesden. In common with other BR standard locomotives, the 9F's were designed to be easy to get at where it mattered, thus making life easier for shed staff and enginemen who had to care for them.

RIGHT: Smokebox cleaning was always one of the dirtiest jobs at an MPD. Accumulated soot and ash had to be raked and shovelled out, and although various mechanical methods were tried over the years, none was really successful, and this remained a chore right to the end of steam. Like *Queen Mary*, No.46126 will have to wait to be cleaned till she returns home, to Carlisle Upperby. She was withdrawn in October 1963.

ALLOCATIONS at CAMDEN (1B) August 1959				
Diesels	**Jubilee 4-6-0**	**Royal Scot 4-6-0**	**Princess 4-6-2**	**3F 0-6-0T**
D210	45592	46100	46207	47302
D211	45599	46101	Total 1	47304
D219	45606	46118		47307
D3847	45624	46135	**Coronation 4-6-2**	47495
D3848	45632	46144	46221	47514
D3849	45669	46146	46229	47522
D3850	45676	46154	46239	47529
Total 7	45686	46161	46240	47668
	45722	46162	46242	47669
	45735	46163	46245	47671
	Total 10	46168	46247	Total 10
		46170	46245	
		Total 12	46256	
			Total 9	
		Patriot 4-6-0		
		45522		
		45523		
		45514		TOTAL STEAM 45
		Total 3		TOTAL DIESEL 7

To the Southern went the distinction of being the last region of British Railways to operate main line express steam. A pleasant paradox when it is remembered that the Southern Railway, and two of its pre-grouping constituent companies, the LB&SCR and the LSWR, were enthusiastic pioneers of electric traction.

At Grouping, the Southern Railway inherited a motley bunch of sheds. Many were small and cramped and most were in urgent need of modernisation. Over the years improvements were made; a considerable number of old sheds were closed, new ones built and some modernised. However, by 1935, work on steam sheds had slowed markedly in anticipation of the complete third rail electrification of the system. However, the war put an end to electrification plans for the time being and then Nationalisation was on the horizon. Still, the old SR did introduce some improvements towards the end of its existence, notably the installation of 70 ft powered turntables at a number of sheds.

After Nationalisation, however, little more was done and the Southern steam MPDs, in common with the rest of BR's sheds, commenced their gradual decline. Any ideas anyone may have had for making steam depots more efficient or better places to work were finally quashed when the Modernisation Plan appeared in 1955, and thereafter the rot really set in.

In the mid-1960's, the south of England became one of the last strongholds of steam in Great Britain. Sheds like Nine Elms, Eastleigh, Basingstoke and others survived to the very end and became probably the most visited and photographed MPDs of all time.

On the Southern

FACING PAGE: Rebuilt Bulleid Merchant Navy Pacific No.35028 *Clan Line* having her smokebox cleaned beside the characteristically Great Western coaling stage at Weymouth shed. Originally built in 1948, rebuilt in 1959 and withdrawn in July 1967, *Clan Line* is now, happily, preserved. The original Southern shed at Weymouth was closed in January 1939. Southern Railway locos were, thereafter, serviced at the Great Western shed where this picture was taken. Weymouth shed (GW) opened in 1885 and finally closed its doors in July 1967.

BELOW LEFT: The brake block of a rebuilt Bulleid Pacific in the last days of steam. Except in a few notable depots, standards of cleaning had drastically declined. You simply could not get the staff. Enginemen found that a good coating of greasy muck on exposed parts actually helped to keep them in good condition. So, if you could not clean an engine really thoroughly, you deliberately left some parts suitably protected like this.

BELOW RIGHT: Another Bulleid Pacific, West Country Class No.34044 *Woolacombe* being turned on the 65 ft power operated turntable at Bournemouth shed. The Southern Railway had completely rebuilt the old shed in the mid thirties, so Bournemouth was relatively modern, if a little cramped. In the last days of steam, it became a Mecca for enthusiasts, before final closure at the same time as Nine Elms, in July 1967.

All photos: Mike Esau

ABOVE: A trio of rebuilt Bulleid Pacifics on the pits outside the Old Running Shed at Nine Elms. This structure dated back to 1885 and the New Shed, the roof of which is just visible to the right, was constructed in 1910. Battle of Britain Class No.34058 *Sir Frederick Pile* is just about to leave. Withdrawn in October 1964, 34058 was still at Barry in the middle of 1980.

Nine Elms was the very last main line steam shed in the London area. The exit road from the coaling plant had a slight upward gradient and Pacifics often had trouble 'getting out from under'. Visitors will remember the fuss and slipping which used to go on when the track became a little greasy.

RIGHT: Basingstoke shed was another outpost a steam, remaining open until 1967. It had the advantage of being easily observable from a nearby main road. In this 1965 picture, a young enthusiast admires BR Standard Class 5 No.73092 and Rebuilt West Country No.34024 *Taw Valley*. The LSWR opened the shed in 1905. A much older shed dating back to 1850 and belonging to the GWR was closed in 1950, after which visiting Western Region engines were serviced at the Southern shed. *Photo: Mike Esau*

Reading, Southern Shed, here potrayed in 1962, was a quiet backwater, typical of many small MPD's throughout the Southern system.

The Reading, Guildford and Reigate Company were responsible for the interesting cross country route between Reading and Redhill. However, the South Eastern Railway bought the RG&R in 1852 and built the small three road brick shed at Reading in the 1850's. Improvements were made in the early 1930's and the shed reached its zenith with an allocation of over twenty engines. It was situated close to the old Reading South Station and the entrance was just off Vastern Road.

ABOVE: There were often interesting visitors to Reading Southern shed. In this picture two U Class 2-6-0's flank 700 Class 0-6-0 No.30690. The 700's were a Drummond design, dating back to 1897 and known to railwaymen as 'Black Motors'. As late as 1960, 28 were still surviving. No.30690 was based at Guildford where she ended her days, being withdrawn in December 1962 and scrapped at Eastleigh in February or March of 1963. The U Class originated as rebuilds of the ill-fated

Maunsell SE&CR River Class 2-6-4T's. The two above, No.31633 (right) and 31625, were originally built as moguls. No.31625 dates from March 1929, was withdrawn in January 1964 and, after a long sojourn at Barry, was bought privately for use on the Mid-Hants Railway where she arrived in March 1980.

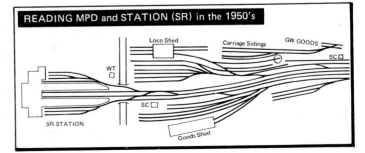

READING MPD and STATION (SR) in the 1950's

Reading SR

ABOVE: Guildford-based N Class 2-6-0 No.31871, carrying the Tonbridge—Reading route headcode, about to leave Reading SR Shed.

TOP RIGHT: Guildford-based U Class 2-6-0 No.31631 being pushed around by her driver and fireman on the manually operated 65 ft turntable at Reading (SR) shed in 1962. The little MPD had just become a sub-shed to Guildford and so had no official loco allocations.

BOTTOM RIGHT: Coaling at its most basic. Here, at the coaling stage, the coal-man is replenishing the tender of N Class 2-6-0 No.31864, a visitor from Redhill. Hand coaling like this survived at many small sheds right to the end of steam.

Reading South Shed closed in January 1965 and on 5th April 1965 Reading South Station also closed. Southern Region operations were all transferred to Reading General Station.

The N's handled much of the passenger traffic between Reading and Redhill for many years. The sole survivor of the class, No.31874, has been restored from scrap and works on the Mid-Hants Railway.

Doncaster Works

Doncaster Works was built for the Great Northern Railway in 1853. Known familiarly as 'The Plant', the works grew from their original 11½ acres to cover 84 acres by 1926. When the Plant Centenary was celebrated in 1953, Doncaster Works employed 3000 people at the locomotive works and 2000 in the carriage and wagon works. It looked after 1300 engines, mostly from the Eastern and North Eastern Regions. 700 locomotives, 2500 carriages and 7500 goods waggons were repaired each year.

In the early days, locomotives were repaired at the GNR's workshops at Boston and originated from a variety of sources, including Sharp Brothers, Hawthorn's and E.B. Wilson & Co. It was not until 1867 that the first engine was actually built at Doncaster. From then until 1957, when steam building ended, Doncaster constructed 2223 engines, including some of the most famous locomotives of all time.

In 1870, the first of Stirling's 8 ft Singles emerged. Ivatt Atlantics were built there, the first large boilered version coming out of shops in 1902. Later, Gresley's Pacifics, including Flying Scotsman, Silver Link and Mallard appeared. The first UK dining car was built at the works in 1879. In 1882, the first British side-corridor coach was designed and built there. In 1921, Gresley's quintuple articulated train set appeared and contained the first all-electric kitchen car. Doncaster built all the special stock for the 'Flying Scotsman' trains, the 'Silver Jubilee' trains of 1935 and, in 1937, the two special sets for the 'Coronation' service between London and Edinburgh.

The last steam locomotive repair carried out at Doncaster was in November 1963, when A4 No.60009 Union of South Africa passed through 'The Plant'. She was withdrawn in June 1966 and is privately preserved.

TOP RIGHT: 'The Plant's'' old main gate. the building on the right was the old, and later the 'new' turnery. On the left is the original erecting shop.

BOTTOM RIGHT: Mr J. C. Sparke, Doncaster Works Manager in the office H.N. Gresley occupied between 1911 and 1922. After Grouping, Gresley's office was off Platform 10 at King's Cross. Wintour, Reeves and Peppercorn all used the office shown here.

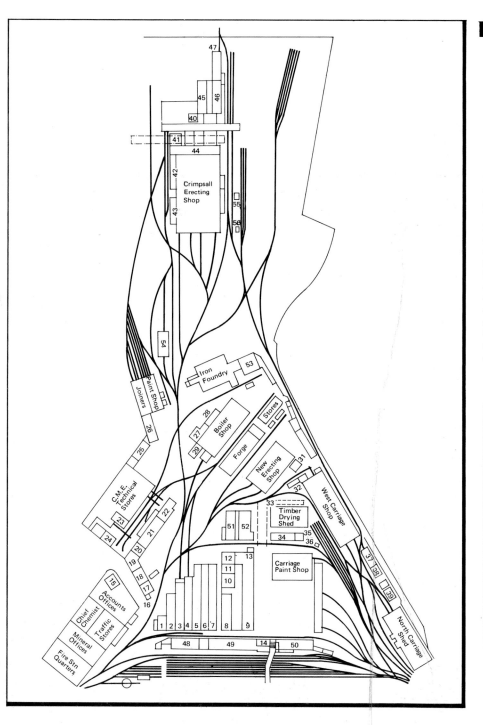

DONCASTER WORKS in the 1950's

1. Out-station office 2. Rods 3. Machining of cylinders 4. Milling, planing, slotting, etc. 5. Turning 6. D shop brass work 7. Frame bay 8. New machine shop 9. Smith's shop 10. Machine-fitter's shop 11. White metal 12. Grinding shop 13. Arc welding 14. Coaching control office 15. Library 16. Fire-engine house 17. Inspection office 18. Hydraulic office 19. Electricity office 20. Electric shop 21. Rubber pipe repair 22. Brass foundry 23. Offices 24. Technical Stores Office 25. Ambulance and first aid room 26. Electric sub-station 27. Flanging shop 28. Boiler shop stores 29. Angle shop 30. Tinsmiths 31. Stores 32. Tyre shed 33. Timber stack 34. Saw mill 35. Timber shed 36. Spray shop 37. Carriage gas shop 38. Stores 39. Tank house 40. Steaming shed 41. Tyre shed 42. Tube house 43. Store 44. Wheel shop 45. Tube repair 46. Engine stripping shop 47. Overhead crane 48. Offices 49. Central drawing office 50. C.M.E. offices 51. Spring shop 52. Plate fabrication 53. Pattern shop 54. Weigh house 55. Air compressors 56. Weigh bridge

Doncaster works plate fitted to *Flying Scotsman*, undeniably the most famous locomotive built at 'The Plant'.

3 4   1 2

1 Rivetters at work on a Pacific's boiler in the Boiler Shop. Note the characteristic 'banjo' dome.

2 Doncaster was one of the few works to have a separate Paint Shop. Here, finishing touches are being applied to the lining out of an A1's boiler. Post-Nationalisation painting of BR locos was on the austere side but 'The Plant' was always able to maintain its own very high standards.

3 A steel tyre, heated by an array of gas jets, about to be shrunk onto the wheel centre of a loco pony truck. Doncaster bogies always had ten-spoked wheels while those made at Darlington had twelve.

4 A4 Pacific No.60028 *Walter K. Whigham* outside the Weigh House. This would have been the Pacific's first steaming after coming out of shops. Here, checks are made for leaks and any weighing and necessary balancing carried out. Then there would be a trial run, followed by a return to the Weigh House for any final adjustments. Note the attachment on the engine headlamp. It bore the legend: 'Return to Doncaster Weigh House.'

5 Crimpsall Erecting Shop. Visible are A3 Pacific No.60111 *Enterprise*, B1 No.61200 and A3 Pacific No. 60100 *Spearmint*.

6 Brake blocks being cast in the Iron Foundry. Note the weights being used to keep the two halves of the mould together during casting.

7 Inside Machine Shop D. The inside cylinder casting of a Thompson 3-cylinder loco is being set up on one of the boring machines.

8 In the Spring Shop a red-hot spring collar is being tapped into position on a leaf spring held together in a spring vice. When cool, it will shrink tightly into place.

5

6

7 8

LEFT: Inside the Wheel Shop at the back of the Crimpsall erecting shop at Doncaster there was always an incredible assortment of wheels of every conceivable shape and size. A mono-rail crane can be seen on the left. Note the set of holes drilled out of the balance weights in the pair of driving wheels on the right. These were concerned with fine balancing. Note, too, the squared milled end of the crank pin. This is to take the eccentric crank which operates the valve gear.

RIGHT: The Engine Stripping Shop was also behind the Crimpsall. Locomotives coming in for a major overhaul were completely taken to pieces and their component parts distributed to various parts of the works for repair or replacement. Eventually, everything was put back together again. This K3, No.61974 from Colwick, has already lost her wheels and her boiler will not be long in coming off.

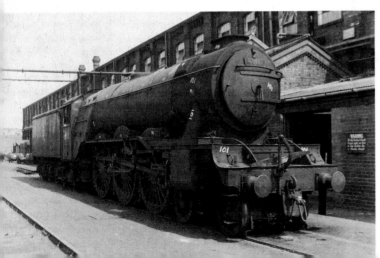

LEFT: A3 Pacific No.60101 *Cicero*, from Haymarket, waits cold outside the Stripping Shop for the beginning of her heavy repair. Every part is clearly labelled with the engine's number so that they are not lost track of in the works. Double-chimneyed Gresley Pacifics would go to Doncaster for major overhaul at about 100,000 mile intervals. Turnaround time would usually be 3-4 weeks. *Cicero* moved to St Margaret's (Edinburgh) in December 1962 and was withdrawn in April 1963, being scrapped a year later.

The Crimpsall erecting shop was added to 'The Plant' in 1901. Here, a Thompson-designed B1 4-6-0, No.61200, is being lowered onto a bogie for valve setting. When this photograph appeared in 'British Railways Magazine - Eastern Region' in October 1960, the editor captioned it, prophetically: "A symphony in metal with the conductor in the fore-ground might well be used to describe this action shot at Doncaster Works. A scene, perhaps, soon to disappear for good."

King's Cross

King's Cross Shed was a grand place. Pride in steam was just as strong there in the last days as it had ever been, and there was a very real enthusiasm and dedication there that were in no small measure responsible for the memorable exploits of the Gresley Pacifics at the end of their outstanding careers.

Beautifully clean engines, lovingly maintained in excellent mechanical condition and manned by some of the country's very best top link crews — those were the hallmarks of old 'Top Shed'.

The shed was situated in a very cramped position right in the middle of King's Cross Goods Yard. Access was from York Way but the shed could not be seen from any road or from the GN main line. Passengers on the North London line, however, had a good view of it from passing trains.

Established by the Great Northern in 1850, some of the original buildings were still in every day use right up to the time the shed closed on June 7th 1963.

From the beginning, substantial facilities for maintenance and repair existed at 'Top Shed'. In the late 1800's, heavy repairs were being undertaken, but these ceased in 1902 when improved facilities, including the new Crimpsall erecting shop, became available at Doncaster.

Over the years improvements were made at the depot. The large mechanical coaling plant was built in 1931 and in December 1932 the 70ft vacuum operated turntable was installed. Up to that time, Gresley Pacifics had to turn on the 70ft turntable which had been in operation at King's Cross Station Yard since 1924.

Famous engines allocated to King's Cross MPD included Flying Scotsman, Silver Link and Mallard.

BELOW: A general view across King's Cross MPD in 1958. On the left, staff relax outside the ashpit foreman's office — a popular place at 'Top Shed' where a cup of tea could usually be had. Pacifics can be seen in the distance in front of the running shed. On the left, over an ash pit, is Immingham B1 No.61195. On the right is B17 No.61657 Doncaster Rovers, from March, and on the extreme right Hitchin-based L1 2-6-4T No.67790, just about to run off shed.

FAR LEFT: Entrance to the offices. The weather vane, cut from sheet brass, was in the form of an Ivatt large-boilered Atlantic; now said to grace a farmyard barn 'somewhere in England'.

LEFT: Array of locomotive headboards kept in the entrance to the running shed foreman's office; names to stir the imagination and bring back memories.

BELOW LEFT: In the notice lobby, Driver Ernie Goodchild of King's Cross checks notices before going on duty.

BELOW RIGHT: Staff take a tea break outside the ash pit foreman's office. The happy atmosphere at the shed is very evident in this 1958 photograph.

Standing and back row left to right: G. Hagland (fireman), P. Roberts (fireman), Bill Young (head shunter), W. Pullen (driver), C. Brown (driver), E. Clowes (driver) and another fireman and a shunter. Front row left to right: L. Charles (fireman), J. Macarthur (driver), J. Ball (driver) and D. Manfredi (fireman).

ABOVE: At 'Top Shed', the greatest pride was taken in turning out immaculate engines. Much credit for this went to charge hand cleaner Dick Ball, seen here touching up the shed plate on an A4.

TOP RIGHT: The LNER Steam Instruction Train was really a school on wheels. It was always on the move, touring motive power depots throughout the region. It would spend a few days at each — here it is seen at King's Cross Shed, with Charlie Brown, the Inspector in Charge on this visit. He is just outside the coach containing a class room complete with blackboard and other teaching aids. The train was a great help to railway staff studying for the various examinations which had to be passed at various stages on the promotion ladder.

BOTTOM RIGHT: The Steam Instruction Train contained a magnificent collection of cut-away engine parts and models. There were, for example, fully working models of the Gresley two-to-one valve gear. Just visible in the distance, on the left, is a model of a boiler showing its Robinson superheater details and cut-away vacuum brake equipment can be seen in the left foreground. A group of passed firemen is receiving instruction.

RIGHT: Shed Master Peter Townend chats with Junior Driver Morris Hook outside the running shed. In this 1959 picture, the loco in the background is A4 No.60006 *Sir Ralph Wedgwood*, previously named *Herring Gull*. The original *Sir Ralph Wedgwood* had been written off after an air raid on York in June 1942.

BELOW: In the erecting shop, two fitters discuss running repairs being carried out on A4 Pacific No.60034 *Lord Faringdon*. Note the string of washers and nuts on a piece of wire hanging on the front of the loco and the piston rings on the buffers. The arches in the erecting shop formed a crescent and were part of the first Great Northern shed of 1850. *Lord Faringdon* was built in 1938 at Doncaster and originally named *Peregrine*. She was withdrawn in August 1966 and scrapped at the end of that year by Hughes Bolckows Ltd at North Blyth.

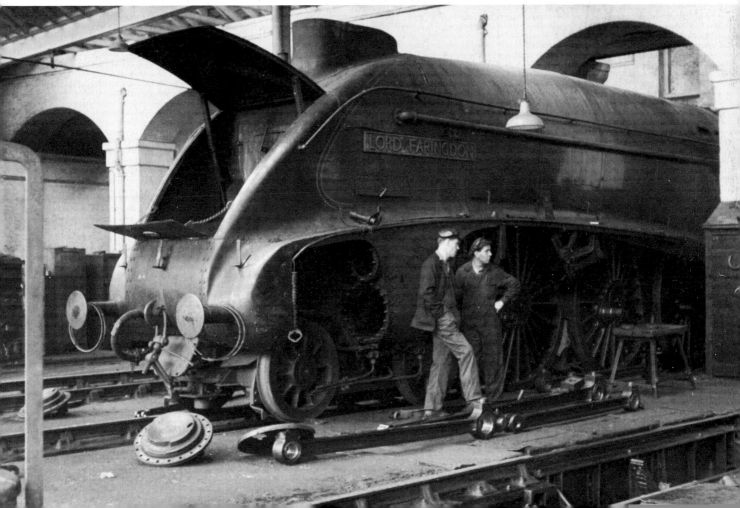

LEFT: Two famous engines at 'Top Shed' in 1958. Fireman Jack Walsh is putting up the light engine lamp for No.60103 *Flying Scotsman* to run down to King's Cross Station to haul the 5.00 pm express to Peterborough. On the left is A4 No.60017 *Silver Fox*, one of the original four streamlined Pacifics built at Doncaster in 1935 to haul the 'Silver Jubilee' trains.

RIGHT: Jack Walsh checks one of 60103's brake blocks. At this time Jack is a passed fireman, preparing to become a driver. The exploits of *Flying Scotsman*, the first Pacific to reach 100 mph, are legendary. Together with No.4476 (later BR 60107) *Royal Lancer*, she inaugurated the non-stop 'Flying Scotsman' on May 1st 1928. Corridor tenders were specially built and fitted to these locos for this service, and later three other Pacifics were similarly equipped.

TOP RIGHT: Driver's eye view from the cab of *Flying Scotsman*, as she starts to ease off shed for the run down to Belle Isle and King's Cross. Driver Pitman of 'Top Shed' is in charge for today's run.

BOTTOM RIGHT: Outside the running shed, an A4 Pacific stands with top streamlined door opened for access to the smoke box door. The detachable hand cranks which operated the streamlined doors were a constant worry to shed staff because they were so easily lost, especially near piles of ash!

On the right, A3 Pacific No. 60059 *Tracery* is almost ready to go off shed to haul the 'Yorkshire Pullman'. The train driver is just getting up into the cab with one of his cans of oil. Made up of several sections, the 'Yorkshire Pullman' provided a luxury service to Doncaster, Leeds, Bradford, Harrogate and Hull and was very popular. No.60059 was built in 1925, withdrawn in 1962 and scrapped at Doncaster in 1963.

H. N. Gresley's original A3 Pacifics, forerunners of the famous A4's, were remarkable engines in their own right. The first, *Great Northern* (No.1470), then designated A1 by the GNR, emerged from Doncaster Works in April 1922.

In BR days, the A3's were classified as 7P, and the A4's 8P. However, after fitting the Kylchap double blast pipe and chimney, the former engines performed so well that they could be seen hauling the East Coast's heaviest and fastest expresses right up to the end of steam.

No.60104 *Solario*, one of the original GNR type Pacifics, built at Doncaster in March 1923, was the first to be withdrawn, in December 1959. The last to go was No.60052 *Prince Palatine*, out of shops at Doncaster in November 1924 and withdrawn during February 1966. Of the 79 original locomotives, only one, *Flying Scotsman*, was preserved.

KING'S CROSS 'TOP SHED' in the 1950's

Diagram labels: Water Softening Plant · Loco Offices · Sand · Lockers · Mess Room · Coal Hoist · Stores · Smithy · Running Shed · Erecting Shop · Boiler House · Turnery · Loco Offices · Met Shed · Loco Building

---

ALLOCATIONS at KINGS CROSS (34A) April 1958

Diesels
12112
13165
13166
13307
13308
13309
13310
13311
13312
13325
13331
13334
D3439
D3440
D3441
D3442
D3443
D3444
D3450
D3473
D3474
D3475
D3490
Total 23

A4 4-6-2
60003†
60006†
60007
60008†
60010
60013
60014
60015
60017
60021
60022
60025
60026†
60028
60029
60030
60032
60033
60034
† non-corridor tender
All ATC fitted
Total 19

A1 4-6-2
60119*
60122
60128
60139*
60149
60156
60157
60158
Total 8

A2 4-6-2
60533
Total 1

A3 4-6-2
60039*
60044
60048
60055
60059
60062*
60066
60103
60108
60109
60110
Total 11

V2 2-6-2
60800
60814*
60820
60854*
60862*
60871
60902
60903*
60914*
60950*
60983*
Total 11

B1 4-6-0
61075
61139
61200
61331*
61364
61393
61394
Total 7

L1 2-6-4T
67757
67768
67770
67773
67774
67776
67779
67784
67793
67794
67797
Total 11

J52 0-6-0ST
68831
68862
Total 2

BR5 4-6-0
73157
73158
73159
Total 3

N2 0-6-2T
69490
69491
69492
69493
69495
69498
69499
69504
69506
69512
69517
69520
69521
69523
69524
69526
69528
69529
69532
69535
69536
69538
69539
69540
69541
69542
69543
69544
69545
69546
69548
69549
69568
69569
69570
69571
69573
69574
69575
69576
69577
69578
69579
69580
69581
69583
69584
69585
69589
69591
69592
69593
Total 52

* ATC fitted

TOTAL STEAM 125
TOTAL DIESEL 23

LEFT: It is Sunday at King's Cross MPD and most of the N2's are at home cold and resting. Amongst those having the day off are Nos. 69549, 69542, 69523 and 69574. No.69523 was withdrawn in 1962 and preserved by the Gresley Society. Restored as LNER No. 4744, she can be seen at Loughborough, the sole survivor of the class.

ABOVE: At the front of King's Cross running shed, a line up of Eastern Region locomotives await cleaning and other attention prior to going on duty later in the day.

RIGHT: B1 Class 4-6-0 No.61096 runs gently onto the turntable. She has just brought one of the 'Cambridge Buffet Expresses' into King's Cross and is visiting 'Top Shed' for servicing before returning to her home depot, Cambridge. The two cylinder B1's were designed by Edward Thompson and introduced in 1942. They were intended to replace many elderly LNER engines, notably GNR Atlantics, and for a time were known as the 'Antelope Class' because the first 41 were named after these animals. Two are preserved at Loughborough. The very popular 'Cambridge Buffet Expresses' started in 1932, being first named 'Garden Cities and Cambridge Buffet Expresses' because of their intermediate stops at Welwyn Garden City and Letchworth. Before the war, they soon became known as 'Beer Trains' and were well patronised for many years.

An N2 0-6-2T under repair at 'Top Shed' in 1958. Note the connections of the condensing apparatus in the smoke box and the superheater elements farther back.

These good looking Gresley tank engines were an improvement on Ivatt's original design. They were general purpose suburban locos and could be found throughout the LNER system. In the London area they handled most of the Great Northern suburban traffic, worked most of the empty express stock in and out of King's Cross Station and could be seen on most of the coal and goods trains on the London suburban branches.

The condensing equipment was for use in working through the underground tunnels to Moorgate, and was fitted or removed as locos were transferred into or away from the London area.

In April 1958, 52 N2's were allocated to King's Cross MPD, all fitted with condensing equipment. Hornsey had 21 (10 without condensers); Hatfield 5 and Hitchin 2, both non-condensing.

In the Met Shed at King's Cross MPD, an N2 Class 0-6-2T, No.69528, undergoes the boiler washout process.

An A1 Pacific has a fault in its sanding gear and a shower of sand falls on the track as fitters sort out the trouble.

In the Met Shed two fitters in the pit under an N2 tank engine.

In the back of the Erecting Shop, A3 No.60107 *Royal Lancer* looks sad after a minor mishap, minus buffers and with a bent front end. She will be repaired shortly at the shed.

In the Blacksmith's Shop. The blacksmith is shaping a brake rod. Note all the tools of the trade hanging up on the wall. This was one of the great crafts — indeed, arts — of the railway industry which vanished with the passing of steam.

The ash pit foreman signals directions to the crew of N2 No.69579, who are waiting to take their loco under the mechanical coaling stage.

A turner operates the big wheel-lathe at 'Top Shed'. He is turning the journal of a pair of driving wheels from a three cylinder locomotive. Note the centre balanced crank which takes the connecting rod driven by the middle cylinder.

Popular Deputy Foreman at King's Cross MPD, Driver J. McArthur, turning a locomotive on the 70 ft vacuum operated turntable. In the background, two N2 tank engines wait to come on shed by passing the turntable. No. 69578 carries the 'Broad Street' headboard.

RIGHT: A team of cleaners hard at work on Peppercorn A1 Pacific No.60149 *Amadis*, one of the eight A1's based at 'Top Shed' in April 1958. She is due to haul the prestigious 'Tees-Tyne Pullman', the post-war successor to the famous 'Silver Jubilee'.

"From cleaning to driving may sometimes appear a long and thorny path to the rising fireman or cleaner, 'ere the responsible position of the locomotive driver is attained" stated an old book on Locomotive Management. Indeed, it was *too* long for many. By 1958, King's Cross MPD was able to recruit staff easily enough but keeping them was another matter.

Amadis was withdrawn in June 1964 and scrapped in January 1965. Sadly, no members of this class were preserved.

FAR RIGHT, TOP: Roller-bearing fitted Peppercorn A1 Pacific No.60157 *Great Eastern* was another of the King's Cross A1's. She amply demonstrated the 'fickle vagaries' of the steam locomotive when she gave persistent trouble with riding, developing such a severe oscillation at around 60 mph that she became hard to fire. Even after stripping down at Doncaster nothing wrong could be found. However, No.60157 returned home 'riding perfectly'. She ended her days at Doncaster Shed (36A), being withdrawn in January 1965 and scrapped at Hull in April of that year.

FAR RIGHT, BOTTOM: In 1959, A4's could often be seen working the 'Tees-Tyne Pullman'. Here the original stream-lined Pacific No.60014 *Silver Link* is about to drop down to King's Cross Station to couple up to the waiting train. Charge Hand Cleaner Dick Ball poses in the foreground. *Silver Link* was specially built for the high speed 'Silver Jubilee' trains which entered service between King's Cross and Newcastle on 30th September 1935. At that time the loco was the only A4 ready, and she gave a most impressive performance, working the train exclusively and clocking up well over 2000 miles a week at high speed without a single failure. This went on for some three weeks before she was joined by the second of the three original A4's. *Silver Link* was withdrawn in December 1962 and cut up at Doncaster in July 1963. Six A4's are preserved.

Epilogue

Steam departed suddenly from Britain's railways. Between 1957 and 1968, over 16,000 locomotives were removed from service, some practically new. In 1959 there were 470 steam sheds. Today there are only 110 motive power depots.

The real demise of steam was even more rapid than the figures suggest. The Southern Region, mainline steam's last stronghold, held out longer than other places because it was considered better to complete the third rail electrification of most of the system *before* withdrawing the steamer. Elsewhere, steam was virtually finished between 1963 and 1964.

The Modernisation Plan published in 1954 was a sensible document, providing for the long term replacement of steam with electric and diesel power, with the accent on the former. It provided, too, for a proper three year test period of a number of makes and types of diesel locomotive and the properly phased transition from steam to other forms of traction *area by area*, so that the correctly foreseen complications of different forms of motive power working side by side could be avoided.

In 1956, however, the British Transport Commission, headed (naturally) by non-railwaymen, decided on the abandonment of the trial period and the wholesale ordering of diesels to replace steam as soon as possible. The reason was political. British Railways were, as ever, in financial trouble and the politicians thought that getting rid of the steam locomotive was the magic solution. They went ahead *contrary to the strongest possible advice from their own highly skilled and experienced experts.*

The result of the BTC's policy is now history and is still the subject of much controversy. Did steam really need to go so quickly? Wasn't it a waste that new and modern steam engines should be scrapped with thirty or more years of useful life left in them? Was it really impossible to get staff to work with steam? Could modern methods have improved steam engine performance and maintenance to reduce substantially pollution and unpleasant working conditions?

Whatever the answers to these questions may be, tha facts are that immense sums spent on purchasing diesel locos meant that the original plans for electrification and other aspects of modernisation have been put back by decades. It is worth remembering, too, that a relatively simple modification — the fitting of the Kylchap double blast pipe and chimney — transformed both the performance and care of many steam engines, notably the A3's and A4's of the ER and the Castles and Kings of the WR. In 1962, these modifications cost only around £200 per locomotive!

Of course, it must be remembered that these policy decisions were made back in the halcyon days of cheap, free-flowing oil. Suez sounded a warning but no one heeded it.

Diesels came in and steam went out. Men, brought up on the whole gamut of arts, crafts and trades surrounding the relatively simple and rugged steam engine, were expected to master overnight all the complexities of the internal combustion engine. Steam engine drivers with only a few hours experience on diesels found themselves attending crash courses so that they could become *instructors* in driving diesels! Small wonder that problems developed.

An what of the transformed BR? Would it be better off today if the original Modernisation Plan had been followed and less money wasted in precipitate dieselisation? Is it purely nostalgic to yearn for the old days, when a couple of Gresley teak corridor coaches could be quickly added to the 'Flying Sctsman', or when *good value for money* refreshments could be had at every seat on 'The Queen of Scots'?

GONE BUT NOT FORGOTTEN
The sheds described in this book

Reading Shed (81D)
Opened 1880. Closed January 1965. There is a diesel depot there now but most of the site is occupied by a new track pre-assembly depot shifted from Theale.

Old Oak Common Shed (81A)
Opened March 17th 1906. Closed to steam March 22nd 1965. Most of the buildings were demolished. Now the site is occupied by a diesel shed and maintenance depot. One turntable of the original four remains.

Camden Shed (1B)
Opened 1847. Closed to steam September 9th 1963. Buildings demolished in 1964. After electrification, sidings on the site used for stabling EMU's.

Weymouth Shed (71G)
Opened 1885. Closed July 1967. Nothing remains. Weymouth is now just a stabling point for two or three diesels.

Bournemouth Shed (71B)
Opened in 1885. Closed July 1967. Site cleared and few traces remain. There is an EMU Depot at Bournemouth.

Nine Elms Shed (70A)
Opened c.1848. Last main line steam shed remaining open in London area. Closed in July 1967. Site completely cleared.

Basingstoke Shed (70D)
Opened in 1905. Closed to steam in 1967. Completely demolished in 1969.

Reading Southern Shed Sub to Guildford
Opened early 1850's. Closed in January 1965. The site cleared and redeveloped. Now occupied by offices and car park.

Doncaster Works
Opened 1853. Now part of British Rail Engineering Ltd.

King's Cross Shed (34A)
Opened in 1850. Closed June 1963. Site cleared and levelled soon after closure. No trace remains.

King at Old Oak Common

N2 at King's Cross